D'Nealian Handwriting

4

Written by Donald Neal Thurber

Scott Foresman
is an imprint of

Editorial Offices: Glenview, Illinois • Parsippany, New Jersey • New York, New York
Sales Offices: Boston, Massachusetts • Duluth, Georgia • Glenview, Illinois • Coppell, Texas
Sacramento, California • Mesa, Arizona

Acknowledgments

Illustrations

Cindy Brodie 42, 90; Rondi Collette 35; Laura D'Argo 9, 28, 91; Joshua Gorchov 76; Judith Love 31; Linda Hawkins 92; Gary Hoover 80, 85; Yoshi Miyaki 19, 55, 70 (bottom), 71; Deb Morse 68; James Needham 86; Kate Pagni (calligraphy) 36, 70, 71; Gary Phillips 73, 75; Cindy Salans-Rosenheim 34; Lauren Scheuer 57, 93; Jeff Severn 38, 53; Georgia Shola 6, 27, 50, 66, 82; Ken Spieling 20, 21, 74; Carol Stutz 56, (lettering) 16, 18, 19, 30, 40, 52, 54; Susan Swan 12, 17 (right); Andrea Tachiera 32, 81; Darcy Whitehead 3, 4, 5, 8, 11, 12, 16, 17, 22, 23, 60, 61, 63, 70 (top), 87

Photographs

Every effort has been made to secure permission and provide appropriate credit for photographic material. The publisher deeply regrets any omission and pledges to correct errors call to its attention in subsequent editions.

Unless otherwise acknowledged, all photographs are the property of Scott Foresman, a division of Pearson Education.

Photo locators denoted as follows: Top (T), Center (C), Bottom (B), Left (L), Right (R), Backaground (Bkgd).

10 (t-b) ©Mark Herreid/Fotolia.com; ©JLV Image Works/Fotolia.com; **14** ©nito/Fotolia.com; **19** ©Amy Myers/fotolia.com; **65** ©Daniel Seidel/Fotolia.com; **72(t-b)** ©Andre/Fotolia.com; ©Johnny Lye/Fotolia.com; **77** Reprinted by permission of United Features Syndicate, Inc.; **88** ©Eric Isselée/Fotolia.com; **89** ©Rick Carlson/Fotolia.com.

D'Nealian® Handwriting is a registered trademark of Donald Neal Thurber

ISBN-13: 978-0-328-21200-2
ISBN-10: 0-328-21200-8

21   17

Table of Contents

Unit Three Applying Handwriting Skills

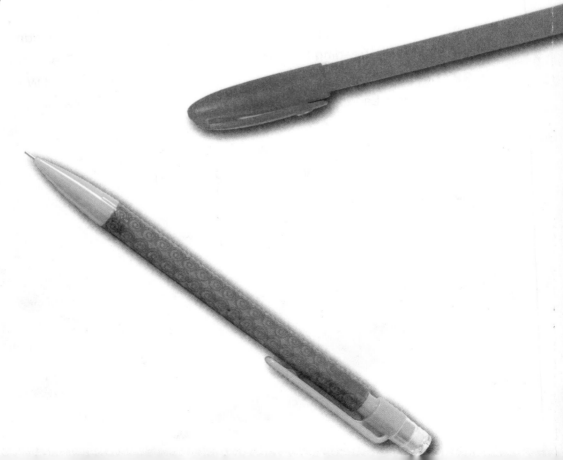

Unit One

Reviewing Manuscript Letters

Reviewing Lower-case Manuscript Letters

Write a row of each lower-case letter.

a

b

c

d

e

f

g

h

i

j

k

l

m

n

o

p

q

r

s

t

u

v

w

x

y

z

Tim's class watched special events at school and went on field trips. Write the class's favorites in manuscript.

harmonica players

dancing puppets

wild animal trainers

backstage at a theater

tour of old airplanes

Reviewing Capital Manuscript Letters

Write a row of each capital letter.

A   J   S

B   K   T

C   L   U

D   M   V

E   N   W

F   O   X

G   P   Y

H   Q   Z

I   R

Stephanie's class always plans a special event for Friday. On Thursday, they put a reminder card on the bulletin board. Write the reminders below in manuscript.

Furry Visitors Hour

Invention Time

Green Eggs Day

Musical Showtime

Health Nut Snack

Reviewing Numbers

Write a row of each number.

1   *6*

2   *7*

3   *8*

4   *9*

5   *10*

When you write a number of more than three figures, use a comma [,] to separate hundreds from thousands.

Jackie hopes she will attend these festivals someday. She looked up how many miles she would have to travel from her home in Detroit.

102
3,768

Write Jackie's notes.

716 miles to Milwaukee

1,211 miles to Cheyenne

1,747 miles to Albuquerque

Making a Bookplate

Clarence reads and collects adventure books. When he lends one to a friend, he pastes a bookplate inside the front cover. He found that the bookplate is a reminder for people to return the book. Look at his bookplate below.

You'll be
a real hero
if you return
this book to
Clarence Johnson
555-8740

In the space below, copy Clarence's bookplate or create one of your own. Use manuscript writing. Plan ahead and adjust your writing to fit the space. Add artwork if you like.

Writing a Message

Hiro lives near the ocean. When he sees large boats in the harbor, he becomes curious about the distant lands they go to. He decided to try to communicate with someone far away, so he wrote a message, put it in a bottle, and threw it into the ocean.

Read Hiro's message below. He planned his writing so that there was enough space between words and sentences.

> August 10, 200_
>
> Hello!
>   My name is Hiro Yamamoto. I am 10 years old and I live at 349 Noyes Street, San Diego, CA 92109. I like to make model ships and learn about foreign lands.
>   Please write and tell me where you found this message.
>
>   Sincerely,
>   Hiro

In manuscript, write a message that you would like someone in another country to read. Leave enough space between words and sentences. Remember to write in a straight line, since there are no writing lines.

Look at the message you wrote. Is there enough space between words and sentences?

Unit Two

Writing Cursive Letters

Writing Cursive lL, hH, and kK

Write a row of each lower-case letter. Be sure to
- touch the top line with the uphill stroke.
- keep the loops open.

Notice where the capital letters **L**, **H**, and **K** touch the top line. Write a row of each letter.

Capital Letter Link-ups
Remember that **L** and **K** join the letters that follow them. Trace the joined letters in the box.

H does not join the letter that follows it. Trace **Ha.**

| *La Ki* |
| *Ha* |

Write the following phrases.

John Hancock Lookout Deck

Hillside Lake Kite Day

Writing Cursive tT, iI, and uU

Write a row of each lower-case letter. Be sure to
- cross **t** and dot **i.**
- make **i** and **u** half as tall as **t.**

Notice where the capital letters **T, I,** and **U** touch the top line. Write a row of each letter.

 Capital Letter Link-ups
Remember that **I** and **U** join the letters that follow them. Trace the joined letters in the box.

T does not join the letter that follows it. Trace **Th.**

Write the following phrases.

Union Train Museum

Island School Talent Show

Writing Cursive eE, jJ, and pP

Write a row of each lower-case letter. Be sure to
- dot **j**.
- keep the loop open in **e**.

Notice where the capital letters **E, J,** and **P** touch the top line. Write a row of each letter.

Capital Letter Link-ups

Remember that **E** and **J** join the letters that follow them. Trace the joined letters in the box.

P does not join the letter that follows it. Trace **Pa.**

En   Ju
Pa

Write the following names of events.

Early American Toys Display

Jacob Lawrence Art Project

Practice

Some letter combinations appear more often than others. Write a row of each pair of letters. Be sure to

- write **l** and **k** with a loop.
- write **t** without a loop.

le
th
lk

le
th
lk

Now write the proper names and sentences below. Be sure to write **l** and **k** with a loop. Write **t** without a loop.

Wilkie Tower　　*Adler College*

A guide led us as we walked through the tower.

We laughed and talked in the crowded elevator.

Some people relaxed near the fountain on the ground level.

Review

Remember that you join capital letters **L, K, I, U, E,** and **J** to the lower-case letters that follow them. Write these names.

Luellen

Kyle

Ileana

Ursula

Eloise

Jake

Remember that you do not join capital letters **H, T,** and **P** to the lower-case letters that follow them. Write the names of these cities.

Hopewell

Tupelo

El Paso

Spot a Problem

Tell why the cursive words below are hard to read.

like

like

pull

puee

Now write **like** and **pull** so that they are easy to read.

Write the following phrase. Make sure your tall letters touch the top line.

from the top of a tall building

Evaluation

Read the hints. Then write the paragraph below. Make your handwriting easy to read.

Hints for Clear Handwriting
- Join lower-case letters.
- Make your tall letters touch the top line.

Our class went to the top of the Hancock Building. The day was clear. We watched sailboats on the sparkling lake and cars snaking down crowded streets. The view was great in every direction!

Check Your Handwriting

Is your handwriting improving? Use the marks below to check the paragraph you wrote.

In the first sentence, **circle** lower-case letters that are not joined.

In the second sentence, **write a check mark above** tall letters that do not touch the top line.

On the lines below, write the number of marks you made.

○ _____   √ _____

Low scores mean your handwriting is easy to read!

Is Your Writing Legible?

Is your handwriting legible or does it look like a secret code? A secret code is impossible to figure out without any clues. Make sure you give your reader all the clues when you write. Check for the following points in your handwriting.

Letter Size and Proportion

Your writing will be easy to read if your letters are the correct size. Look at the letters at the right. The small letters are half the size of the tall letters. The tall letters touch the top line. Letters with descenders go below the bottom line.

i e u
l h k
j p g

Write your name below. Concentrate on making your letters the correct size.

Letter Form

Can you read the word below? The word is **outing.** Why is it hard to read?

iuling

Write **outing** correctly. Remember to close **o**, cross **t**, and dot **i.**

Write the name of one of your classmates. Concentrate on forming your letters correctly.

Now ask that classmate to read the name. Does he or she think it's legible?

Letter Slant

Your handwriting will be easy to read if you slant all your letters the same way. Don't worry if your letters slant in a different direction from your classmate's. Write the name of your school below.

_____

_____

Look at the words you wrote. Then look at the examples below. In the space below, write the word or phrase that describes your slant.

right   _left_   _up and down_

_____

_____

Letter and Word Spacing

Be sure that you have the right amount of spacing between letters and words. Don't crowd letters too closely together. Leave more space between words than between letters in a word. Write the question below.

Where are you in the group photo?

_____

_____

Look at the examples below. Then look at the question you wrote. Write the word or phrase that describes the spacing in your handwriting.

even   _too close_

too far apart

_____

Using Proofreading Marks

In the paragraph below, Rita used proofreading marks to show how she wanted to correct her copy. The proofreading marks and what they mean are shown at the right. Notice how Rita corrected her copy. Look at the position of each mark.

	Proofreading Marks
≡	Make a capital letter.
∧	Add a word or words.
ⓢⓟ	Correct the spelling.
⊙	Add a period.
⑦	Add a question mark.
⑴	Add an exclamation mark.
ℓ	Take out a word or words.

Do you like stories⑦
what I like
Mysteries are ∧best. I
ⓢⓟ   ⓢⓟ read
red one to my ~~my~~
really
sister. she was ∧scared!

Write a neat final copy of Rita's paragraph. Make the corrections shown by the proofreading marks. You do not have to skip lines. Use cursive writing.

_____

_____

_____

_____

Look at what you wrote. Did you make all the corrections? Does your writing look neat?

Read the paragraph below. Notice the mistakes. Use the proofreading marks on page 20 to show how the paragraph should be corrected.

The book is abot Cam—a detective with the a great memory. She new there should 34 bones in the dinosaur's skeleton. but she saw only 31

In the space below, write the paragraph as a final copy. Make the corrections shown by the proofreading marks. You do not have to skip lines. Use cursive writing.

Read what you wrote. Did you make all the corrections? Does the paragraph make sense?

Timed Writing

Tom's teacher gave the students four minutes before the end of class to copy the instructions for an assignment. Read the assignment below.

> ### Language Assignment
> Look through newspapers and magazines. Cut out pictures of three animals you think are interesting. Write three sentences. Tell why you liked each animal. Leave enough space after each sentence so that you can paste the animal's picture near it. Turn in the paper tomorrow.

When you have to write quickly, use these tips.
- First, read what you have to copy. Think about how you can write it in a shorter form and still include all the important information.
- Use manuscript or cursive, whichever you write faster.
- When you write, skip words that are not important.

Write Tom's assignment in the space below. Time your writing. Use a clock, a timer, or have a friend time you. Stop writing when four minutes are up.

_____

_____

_____

_____

_____

_____

Now read what you wrote. Do you understand the assignment? Did you remember to write when it is due?

Writing for a Test

Good handwriting helps you do your best when you write for a test.
Good handwriting makes your answers easier to read.
Good handwriting helps you communicate your ideas more clearly.
Good handwriting helps you answer test questions within a specified amount of time.

Getting Ready
- Read the test prompt carefully.
- Think about what you want to write.

Writing a Response
- Plan your writing by organizing your ideas.
- Express your ideas clearly and completely.
  Support your ideas with details or examples.
  Choose words that will help others understand what you mean.
  Use correct grammar, spelling, punctuation, and paragraphs.
- Use your best handwriting.
  Letters should not be too close together or too far apart.
  Letters should be the correct size and proportion to fit the space given.
- Review and edit your writing.
  Use proofreading marks to make corrections or erase carefully and rewrite.

Everyone has tried something new at one time or another. Think about a time you tried something new. Now write a story about that time.

I remember a time wen I (sp) when was in third grade I had never been to a baseball game before. Can you believe that(?)

Here is a writing prompt and Marisa's answer.

> Everyone has jobs or chores. Think about one of your jobs or chores. Now explain why you do your job or chore.
>
> Last year we got a cat named Whiskers and he is white with black paws and he is very frendly. My little sisters job is to feed whiskers every day in the morning. My job is to wash the dishes after dinner every night and in the morning I make my bed before I go to school. If I'm late for school then I make my bed when I get home. I like helping at home.

Look at how Marisa wrote her answer.

	Yes	No
• Is there the same amount of space between each of the letters in her words?	☐	☐
• Did she use correct letter size and proportion?	☐	☐
• Did she fix mistakes carefully?	☐	☐
• Did she organize her ideas well?	☐	☐
• Did she support her ideas with examples or details?	☐	☐

What letters do not have the correct spacing, size, or proportion? Make a line under them. Which ideas do not support Marisa's answer? Cross them out. Which sentence should go first in the paragraph? Circle it.

Now you write a response to the same prompt that Marisa used.

_____

_____

_____

_____

_____

_____

_____

_____

_____

_____

_____

_____

_____

Check your handwriting.   Yes   No

- Is there the same amount of space between
  each of the letters in your words?   ☐   ☐
- Did you use correct letter size and proportion?   ☐   ☐
- Did you fix mistakes carefully?   ☐   ☐
- Did you organize your ideas well?   ☐   ☐
- Did you support your ideas with examples
  or details?   ☐   ☐

Draw a line under the sentence you wrote best.

Writing Cursive aA, dD, and cC

Write a row of each lower-case letter. Be sure to
- close **a** and **d.**
- keep **c** open.

Notice where the capital letters **A, D,** and **C** touch the top line. Write a row of each letter.

Capital Letter Link-ups
Remember that **A** and **C** join the letters that follow them. Trace the joined letters in the box.

D does not join the letter that follows it. Trace **Dr.**

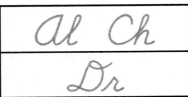

Write the following names of events.

Young American Authors Day

Drummers and Dancers Concert

Writing Cursive nN, mM, and xX

Imagine that there is a dotted line halfway between each of the lines below. Write a row of each lower-case letter. Make **n, m,** and **x** touch the imaginary midline.

Notice that capital letters **N, M,** and **X** have the same beginning stroke. Write a row of each letter.

Capital Letter Link-ups

Remember that **N** and **M** join the letters that follow them. Trace the joined letters in the box.

X does not join the letter that follows it. Trace **Xa**.

> No Mi
> Xa

Write the following names of events.

Newport News Music Festival

Lake Xochimilco Mural Opening

Writing Cursive gG, yY, and qQ

Write a row of each lower-case letter. Be sure to
- swing the bottom loop of **g** and **y** to the left.
- swing the bottom loop of **q** to the right.

Notice that capital letters **Q** and **Y** start near the top line.
G starts at the bottom line. Write a row of each letter.

 Capital Letter Link-ups
Remember that **Y** and **Q** join the letters that follow them.
Trace the joined letters in the box.

G does not join the letter that follows it. Trace **Ga**.

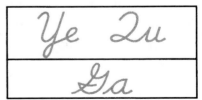

Write the following phrases.

Grafton Square Yoyo Players

Recycling Quart and Gallon Bottles

Practice

Some letter combinations appear more often than others.
Write a row of each pair of letters. Be sure to
- swing the loops of **g** and **y** to the left.
- close **a** and **d.**

dg   *dg*

ay   *ay*

nc   *nc*

Write the proper nouns and the sentences below. Be sure
to swing the loops of **g** and **y** to the left. Close **a** and **d.**

Dance Theater   Ridgeway Woods

Yesterday we went to an outdoor concert at Edgewater Park.

Six children dressed as mice danced over the gray bridge.

Quincy didn't budge during the performance.

Review

Remember that you join capital letters **A, C, N, M, Y,** and **Q** to the lower-case letters that follow them. Write these names.

Audrey _____ **Cooper** _____ **Nancy** _____

_____ _____ _____

Miguel _____ **Yolanda** _____ **Quon** _____

_____ _____ _____

Remember that you do not join capital letters **D, X,** and **G** to the lower-case letters that follow them. Write the names of these cities.

Dexter _____ **Xenia** _____ **Grundy** _____

_____ _____ _____

Spot a Problem

Tell why the cursive words below are hard to read.

voices

voices

fiddle

fiddle

Now write **voices** and **fiddle** so that they are easy to read.

_____ _____

_____ _____

Write the following phrase. Make sure your closed letters are properly formed.

a quartet singing a melody

_____

_____

Evaluation

Read the hints. Then write the paragraph below. Make your handwriting easy to read.

Hints for Clear Handwriting
- Close letters **a** and **d.**
- Use only cursive letters.

On Monday we went on a field trip to Riverside Park. We watched a group of drummers playing exciting rhythms. Afterwards, we took turns playing the drums. I'd like to try that again someday.

Check Your Handwriting

Is your handwriting improving? Use the marks below to check the paragraph you wrote.

In the first sentence, **circle** every **a** and **d** that is not closed.

In the second sentence, **write a check mark** above every letter that is not in cursive.

On the lines below, write the number of marks you made.

○ _____   √ _____

Low scores mean your handwriting is easy to read!

Letter Size and Proportion

Have you seen the small chairs and tables for kindergarten children? In the upper grades, the size of the furniture changes to fit bigger children. Make sure you change, or adjust, your handwriting to fit the size of the writing space.

Write the names on the cards below. Adjust your writing to fit each space. Use manuscript writing.

Missie

Danica

Benny filled in a name tag for his backpack. Some of his numbers bumped into letters with descenders. Copy the information from his name tag in the form below. Make sure each letter has its own space.

This belongs to

Name _Benny King_

Address _5580 S. 79th St. Chicago, IL 60637_

This belongs to

Name

Address

Did you plan well? Is your writing too big, too small, or just about right?

To make sure your letters are the right size, make your tall letters and numbers touch the top lines. Make your small letters half the size of your tall letters.

Look at the letters on the chalkboard at the right. Some of them are the answers to the letter riddles below. Write each riddle and its answer in cursive.

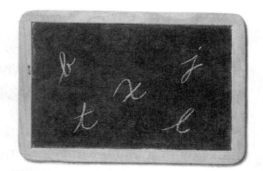

Which letter can you drink?

Which letter is a bird?

Which letter stings?

A teacher and a student wrote the names of two special days at their school. The student used student proportion, but the teacher used adult proportion. Notice that the student's tall letters touch the top line, but the teacher's do not. In both examples the small letters are half the size of the tall letters. This means that both handwriting examples are in correct proportion.

student proportion

Earth Day

adult proportion

Arbor Day

Now write the words below in adult proportion. Make your small letters half the size of the tall letters.

Spaulding School Fun Fair

Making a Business Card

Ruben wants to earn money by baby-sitting and dog-walking in his spare time. When he tells people that he is available, he hands them business cards that he made so they will remember him.

Look at Ruben's business card. Notice that he wrote the kinds of jobs he wants in larger letters. He wrote the rest of the information in smaller letters.

Baby-sitting   Dog-walking

Call Ruben Morales   555–6193

Weekdays, 4:15 – 7:30 p.m.
Saturdays and Sundays, all afternoon

Create your own business card in the space below. Use manuscript writing. Write the job you want in bigger letters. Write the rest of the information in smaller letters. Adjust your handwriting to fit the space.

Look at the card you wrote. If you were going to write a real business card, would you need to change anything?

Solving a Crossword Puzzle

Patti's grandpa made her a birthday card with a crossword puzzle. When she solved it, she found that the words described *her*.

Solve the crossword puzzle below. Because each letter is in its own box, manuscript is more appropriate.

Clues

Down:

1. She will have a *jolly* birthday.
2. She wants to be *a person who puts out flames.*
4. She makes people *giggle*.
5. She likes to *fool* me.

Across:

3. She is a *wonderful* granddaughter.
6. Her favorite sport is *splashing*.
7. She is *five plus five* years old today.

To Patti,

Love,
Grandpa

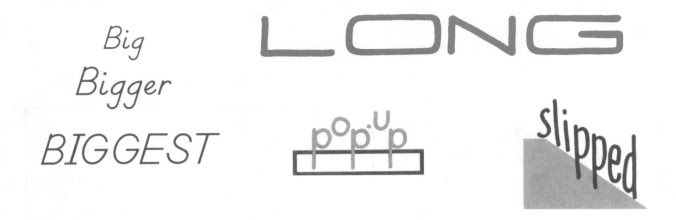

Just by looking at the way those words are written, you can understand what they mean. Pick some words from the list below or think of your own. Then let your imagination go.

Create your own word pictures in the space below. Write the letters so they show the meaning of the word. Would manuscript or cursive handwriting show the meaning better? Would capital or lower-case letters be better?

zero	giraffe	ladder	bubble
butterfly	basketball	tiny	sneeze
snake	strong	bumpy	shadow

Writing Cursive oO, wW, and bB

Write a row of each lower-case letter. Be sure to
- close **o.**
- keep the loop open on **b.**

Notice that capital letters **O** and **B** start at the top line, while **W** starts just below it. Write a row of each letter.

Capital Letter Link-ups

Remember that **O**, **W**, and **B** do not join the letters that follow them.

Trace the letter groups in the box.

On We
Br

Write the following names of events.

Indoor Obstacle Bike Race

"What will I be?" Day

Joining Sidestroke Letters

Look at letters **o** and **n** at the right. Now look at the joined letters in **on.** Notice that
- before joining, the beginning stroke of **n** touches the bottom line.
- after joining, the beginning stroke of **n** does not touch the bottom line.

o   n   on

When you join letters **o, w,** and **b** to other letters, do not touch the bottom line.

ot   wh   br

Write the words and sentences below.

one   work   oboe

who   wobble   bobber

Wesley whispered to the watchful woodchuck.

Belinda ate berries under the branches of a big birch tree.

38

Practice

Some letter combinations appear more often than others.
Write a row of each pair of letters. Be sure to
- keep the loop open on **b**.
- close **o**.
- make **o** and **w** half as tall as **b**.

bl   *bl*
wh   *wh*
ou   *ou*

Now write the names of the places and sentences below.
Be sure your small letters are half the size of your tall
letters.

Coulee Dam   *Pebble Beach*

Bill daydreams about what he'll be and where he'll go someday.

He wonders what he'll be able to do.

He thinks about flying a blimp.

He imagines touring London while riding a double-decker bus.

Review

Remember that you do not join capital cursive letters **O**, **W,** and **B** to the lower-case letters that follow them. Write these names.

Beth

Olivia

Willow

William

Barry

Orville

Remember to make your small letters half the size of your tall letters. Write the names of these American towns.

Woodbury

Boonton

Ottawa

Spot a Problem

Tell why the cursive words below are hard to read.

wish

wish

hope

hope

Now write **wish** and **hope** so that they are easy to read.

Write the following phrase. Use a sidestroke to join **o, w,** and **b** to the letters that follow them.

winning a blue ribbon

40

Evaluation

Read the hints. Then write the paragraph below. Make your handwriting easy to read.

Hints for Clear Handwriting
- Close **o**.
- Keep the loop open on **b**.

Win always notices a sculpture of a little angel on a nearby church. It's made of stone, but it looks soft and chubby. At home, Win makes her own angels out of clay. First she shapes a face and a small body. Then she adds wings.

_____

_____

_____

_____

_____

_____

_____

 Check Your Handwriting

Is your handwriting improving? Use the marks below to check the paragraph you wrote.

In the first sentence, **circle** every **o** that is not closed.

In the second sentence, **write a check mark** near every **b** that does not have a loop.

On the lines below, write the number of marks you made.

○ _____   √ _____

Low scores mean your handwriting is easy to read!

41

Letter Form

It would be hard to ride a bicycle with parts that are not made correctly. It is also hard to read handwriting when the letters are not formed correctly. When you write, make sure letters like **l** and **h** have loops. Cross **t** and dot **i** and **j**.

Jason rode his new bicycle to the library. He wanted the books listed below, but he could not find them on the shelves. Write the titles and authors below. Remember to underline titles of books.

How to Speak Clearly by Whujuh Sey

_____

_____

Yummy Meals by Aunt Eder

_____

_____

101 Excuses by I. M. Lion

_____

_____

Scary Stories by Yell N. Holler

_____

_____

My Life in the Circus by Akro Batt

_____

_____

Look at what you wrote. Did you form your letters correctly?

Letters like the ones at the right are easy to read because they are formed correctly. Cursive **e** is open but **i** is not. Cursive **l** has a loop but **t** does not.

e i

Jason was able to find books about what he likes to do in his spare time. Copy the topics of Jason's books on the lines below.

l t

doodling and painting

_____

acting in skits

_____

collecting fingerprints

_____

Make sure the bottom loops on your descender letters swing in the correct direction. Look at the letters at the right. Cursive **g** and **y** have bottom loops that swing to the left, but **q** has a bottom loop that swings to the right.

g y

Write the sentences below. Think about how to form each letter as you write it.

q

Jason stopped for a while at a display of holograms.

_____

_____

Then he checked out the books and rode quickly home.

_____

_____

Look at your writing. Are the letters formed correctly?

Timed Writing

After choir practice, Mrs. Robinson asked Sheila to give her dad a message. When Sheila got home, she quickly wrote the message down so she wouldn't forget it. The message was on the table when Sheila's dad got home from work. Below, read what Mrs. Robinson told Sheila.

> "Sheila, you know that your dad is organizing a bake sale. Would you tell him that I will not be able to help at the sale on Saturday? I have to go out of town that day, but I'll drop off my bread on Friday. Thanks for your help!"

Use these tips when you write a message for someone else.
- Include important names, dates, and events.
- Use manuscript or cursive, whichever is faster.
- Write in complete sentences so that the message will be easy for the reader to understand.

Decide what parts of Mrs. Robinson's message are important to write down. Then write the message in either manuscript or cursive in the space below. Time your writing. Use a clock, a timer, or have a friend time you. Stop writing when four minutes are up.

_____

_____

_____

_____

_____

_____

_____

Now read what you wrote. Did you write down the names, days, and events?

Writing a Math Test

Good handwriting helps you do well on math tests. Good handwriting makes your numbers and words easy to read.

Getting Ready
- Read the test question carefully.
- Be sure you understand what the question is asking you to do.

Finding the Rule

Fill in the missing output number in the table.
What is the rule?

- Look at the numbers in the input boxes. Figure out what operation you use to change them to output numbers.
- Tell the rule for changing the input numbers.
- Use your best handwriting.
  The size of your handwriting should fit the space in the table.
  All your numbers and letters should slant in the same direction.

Input	Output
8	32
9	36
10	40
11	44

Multiply by 4.

- Review and edit your writing. Use proofreading marks to make corrections or erase carefully and rewrite.

Miguel completed the input/output table below. Then he wrote the rule.

Fill in the missing output number in the table.
Write the rule.

Input	Output
3	9
4	16
5	25
6	3b

Multiply each input numbr by itself.

Look at how Miguel solved the problem.
- Did he adjust his handwriting to fit the table?
- Do his letters and numbers slant the same way?
- Is his handwriting easy to read?

Yes No
☐   ☐

☐   ☐
☐   ☐

Which letters and number do not have the correct slant? Circle them.

Which words are spelled incorrectly? Cross them out and write them correctly on the line above.

Now you find the missing numbers in the table below. Write the rule.

Fill in the missing numbers in the table.
What is the rule?

Input	Output
6	18
	21
8	24
9	

_____

_____

Check your handwriting.

	Yes	No
• Did you adjust your handwriting to fit the table?	☐	☐
• Do your letters and numbers slant the same way?	☐	☐
• Is your handwriting easy to read?	☐	☐
• Did you fix mistakes carefully?	☐	☐

Circle the number you wrote best.

Writing Cursive vV and zZ

Imagine that there is a dotted line halfway between each of the lines below. Write a row of each lower-case letter. Make **v** and **z** touch the imaginary midline.

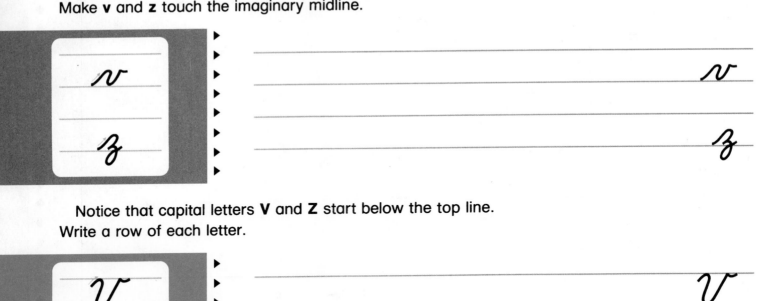

Notice that capital letters **V** and **Z** start below the top line. Write a row of each letter.

Capital Letter Link-ups

Remember that **Z** joins the letters that follow it. Trace the joined letters in the box.

V does not join the letter that follows it. Trace **Vo.**

Write the following names of events.

Riverview Cavern Visit

Vandalia Zoo Trip

Crazy Questions Quiz Show

Writing Cursive sS, rR, and fF

Write a row of each lower-case letter. Be sure to
- keep **r** open.
- close **s.**

Notice that capital **F** has three strokes. Now write a row of each letter.

Capital Letter Link-ups

Remember that **R** joins the letter that follows it. Trace the joined letters in the box.

S and **F** do not join the letters that follow them. Trace **Sa** and **Fr.**

Ro
Sa   Fr

Write these events.

East Rumford Science Fair

Submarine Tour Field Trip

Joining Sidestroke Letters

Look at letters **o**, **w**, **b**, and **v** at the right. They end with sidestrokes. These strokes do not touch the bottom line.

Use a sidestroke when you join **o**, **w**, **b**, and **v** to other letters.

o   w   b   v

of   wr   bu   ve

Write the words and sentences below.

out   *way*   *bobcat*

went   *voter*   *volley*

Vanessa viewed a very lovely valley.

Oscar opened oodles of oysters over by the ocean.

Practice

Some letter combinations appear more often than others.
Write a row of each pair of letters. Be sure to

- write **f** and **h** with loops.
- close **s.**

ve

sh

fr

ve

sh

fr

Now write the proper nouns and the sentences below. Be
sure to keep the loops open in **f** and **h** and close **s.**

Fishing Derby   *Harvest Festival*

*Would you like to have some
outdoor creatures as friends?*

*If you have an old wooden tub,
you can build a fishpond.*

*Add fresh water, plants, and
shells, if you wish.*

Birds, frogs, and snails love ponds!

Review

Remember that you join capital letters **Z** and **R** to the lower-case letters that follow them. Write these names.

Zondra

Rosetta

Rafael

Roger

Zeb

Zeke

Remember that you do not join capital letters **V, S,** and **F** to the lower-case letters that follow them. Write the names of these places.

Sun Valley

Stonington

Fairhaven

Spot a Problem

Tell why the cursive words below are hard to read.

sister

sister

remember

remember

Now write **sister** and **remember** so that they are easy to read.

Write the following phrase. Make sure your small letters are half the size of your tall letters.

rain drizzling on the soft ground

Evaluation

Read the hints. Then write the paragraph below. Make your handwriting easy to read.

Hints for Clear Handwriting
- Close **s.**
- Write **f** with two loops.

Every spring Uncle Russell and I start our garden. We plant colorful flowers, cauliflower, and other vegetables. But we're always chasing away hungry rabbits that eat the plants. Rabbits are fun to watch. How can we have a garden and rabbits too?

Check Your Handwriting

Is your handwriting improving? Use the marks below to check the paragraph you wrote.

In the first sentence, **circle** every **s** that is not closed.

In the second sentence, **write a check mark next to** every **f** that does not have loops.

On the lines below, write the number of marks you made.
◯ _____   √ _____

Low scores mean your handwriting is easy to read!

Letter Slant

Imagine what a tug-of-war would be like if the people on your side pulled in different directions. They would probably bump into each other. When you write, slant your letters in the same direction so they don't bump into each other. Study the sentences below. Then copy the sentence that tells how your writing slants.

It slants to the right.
It slants to the left.
It is straight up and down.

Kate used many punctuation marks in a story she wrote about how she played when she was younger. Copy the following sentences from her story. Slant your letters and punctuation marks in the same direction.

Imagine what we could make out of these huge boxes, some blankets, and a rope!

Let's make holes in the boxes for doors and windows.

We'll call it the "Enchanted Towers."

Remember that numbers must slant in the same direction as the rest of your handwriting.

The children in Kate's story imagined that everything was larger than it really was. Write the following phrases from her story.

Hello, my name is Fido.

200 feet high

10,000 mosquitoes

110 degrees

To make your handwriting easy to read, keep your tall letters from bumping into letters with descenders. Look at the descender letters and tall letters in the paragraph below. Each letter is in its own space. Copy what Kate wrote in her journal.

Today my imagination came in handy. This morning I made up a riddle. In school, I wrote a story, and on the way home, I daydreamed about being an inventor.

Timed Writing

Do you ever read a textbook chapter and then forget what you read? If you take short notes, you will probably remember more.

Use these tips to take notes from a textbook.
- First, read through the part you are assigned.
- Go back and write down important facts, dates, and definitions. Use manuscript or cursive, whichever you write faster.
- Write legibly so you can read the notes at a later time.

Read through the paragraph about steam power below. In the space below, write three or four notes about what you read. Time your reading and note-taking. Use a clock, a timer, or have a friend time you. Stop when four minutes are up.

Steam Locomotive

The coming of steam power. Inventors in England had been working on the steam engine for many years. Finally, in 1769, an Englishman named James Watt built a steam engine that worked well. Now factories could be built anywhere. They no longer needed to be built near water. Steam could be used to power boats, trains, hammers, and pumps.

Can you understand what you wrote? Did you write important facts, dates, and names?

Writing a Language Arts Test

Good handwriting helps you do well on tests. It makes your words easy to read. It helps you communicate your ideas more clearly.

Getting Ready

In a test, you may have to read a passage and answer a question about it by organizing information.

- Read the passage and question carefully.
- Be sure you understand what to do.

Writing a Response

- One test had a passage about water. Here is an example of a web that organizes information from the passage.
- When you write a response, use your best handwriting. Adjust your handwriting to fit the space in the ovals of the web.
- Letters should not be too close together or too far apart.

I need to find four facts about water.

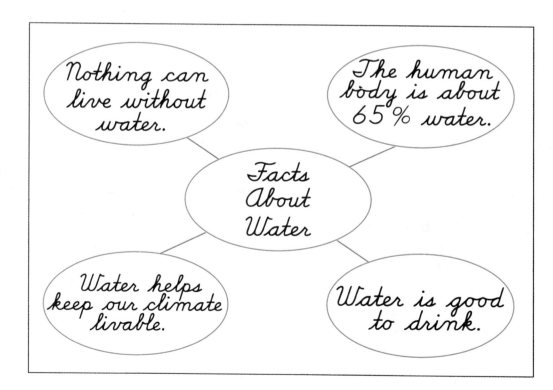

Nothing can live without water.

The human body is about 65% water.

Facts About Water

Water helps keep our climate livable.

Water is good to drink.

- Review and edit your writing. Use proofreading marks to make corrections or erase carefully and rewrite.

Keshia completed a web using the passage below.

Most of Earth's water, about 97 percent, is in the oceans. The remaining 3 percent is fresh water. Most of the fresh water is in glaciers and icecaps. The rest is ground water, rivers, swamps, and lakes. Even though rivers make up a very small percentage of Earth's water, this is where we get most of the water for our everyday use.

What are four facts you learned about Earth's water?
Write your answer in the ovals of the web below.

3 percent is fresh water.

Most water is in the oceans.

Facts About Water

Most fresh water is in glashers and icecaps.

Most water we use every day comes from rivers.

Look at how Keshia answered the question.   Yes   No
- Did she adjust her handwriting to fit the circles?   ☐   ☐
- Is her handwriting easy to read?   ☐   ☐
- Did she fix mistakes carefully?   ☐   ☐

What letters and words are not evenly spaced? Circle them.
Which word is spelled incorrectly? Cross it out and write it correctly above.

Now you complete a web using the information in the passage below.

Did you know that the same water that existed on Earth millions of years ago is still here today? Thanks to the way water moves in and out of Earth's atmosphere, water is continuously being recycled all around the globe. Earth is a "closed system," like a terrarium. This means that very few of Earth's substances, including water, escape into outer space.

What are four facts you learned about Earth's water? Write your answers in the ovals of the web below.

Facts About Water

Check your handwriting.

	Yes	No
• Did you adjust your handwriting to fit the space?	☐	☐
• Is your handwriting easy to read?	☐	☐
• Did you fix mistakes carefully?	☐	☐

Put a check by the fact you wrote best.

Fun with Handwriting: Awards

On most evenings Leticia could hear her brother trying to play the guitar. When he played his first song, she made him an award. Leticia decided to be creative. She used both manuscript and cursive writing to decorate her award.

Now make your own award in the space at the right. Be creative!

Unit Three

Applying Handwriting Skills

Writing the Time

Jenny has to complete the message at the right. She can write the time in one of three ways shown below. The shortest way is to use numbers. When you use numbers, remember to add a colon ⬚ to separate the hours from the minutes. Colons are the same size as lower-case letters.

Chorus practice is today at

quarter past three   *three-fifteen*   *3:15*

Write each time below.

10:15   *8:04*   *5:30*

Use numbers and colons to write each time below. Remember that numbers are the same size as tall letters.

ten minutes past seven _____

twenty minutes past one _____

quarter after eleven _____

When you write the abbreviations **a.m.** and **p.m.,** use lower-case letters and periods.

Write the times below. Next to each time, write what you are usually doing at that time of day.

7:00 a.m.

_____

4:10 p.m.

_____

8:15 p.m.

_____

Making a Schedule

Tanya and her family had to move to a new town. She decided to make a schedule of what she had to do for the week before she moved. To make the schedule, Tanya drew a box and some vertical lines on notebook paper.

Read Tanya's schedule below. Look at the size of the letters. The capital letters do not touch the top line, but the small letters are still half the size of the tall letters. This means the words are written in adult proportion.

Day	Things to Do	Time
Wed.	Dentist	3:30 p.m.
Thurs.	Dinner at Aunt Flossie's	5:30 p.m.
Fri.	Sleepover at Keisha's	6:30 p.m.
Sat.	Pizza lunch with Scouts	11:15 a.m.– 12:45 p.m.
Sun.	Moving day	9:00 a.m.

Copy Tanya's schedule in the form below. Adjust the size of your handwriting to fit the space. Use adult proportion. Keep your small letters half the size of your tall letters.

Day	Things to Do	Time

Writing Addresses

Riki wrote a letter to her dad. She made sure she wrote the words and numbers clearly so the letter would reach her dad's mailbox. Study Riki's envelope and the tips below.

Include a return address.

RIKI FULTON
219 BURR OAK DR
LAFAYETTE IN 47901

MR MARK FULTON
1609 W TYLER ST
ROCHESTER IN 46975

Use all capital manuscript letters and no punctuation marks.

Address the envelope using the information below.

Mailing address: Ray Chasing Hawk, 619 River Road,
                      Yankton, SD 57078

Return address: Jon Hanson, 525 South Hill Road,
                      Baltimore, MD 21230

Can another person read your envelope?

Writing a Postcard

When you write a postcard, your writing must fit into a small space. Look at the words in the postcard below. They are written smaller than usual. Sometimes tall letters are very close to letters with descenders, but they do not bump into each other.

Potawatomi Memorial Village

April 27, 200_

Hi Dan,

   See the wigwam on this card? I sat inside one just like it. An Indian storyteller told us about the tribe's heroes.

Eduardo

DAN HOFFMAN

24 ELM ST APT 18

WHITTIER CA 90609

Copy Eduardo's postcard below. Adjust your writing to fit the space. Make sure your tall letters do not bump into letters with descenders.

Potawatomi Memorial Village

Look at the postcard you wrote. Do your tall letters and letters with descenders fit into their own spaces?

Writing Measurements

Most people abbreviate when they write measurements. Look at the chart below. Only the abbreviation for *inch* has a period. Also, only the abbreviation for *liter* has a capital.

inch	**in.**	ounce	**oz**
foot	**ft**	pound	**lb**
yard	**yd**	pint	**pt**
mile	**mi**	quart	**qt**
centimeter	**cm**	gallon	**gal**
meter	**m**	liter	**L**

Use the same abbreviation for singular and plural measurements.

Rewrite the following measurements in cursive. Use abbreviations for the underlined words.

15 <u>miles</u>

8 <u>inches</u>

26 <u>meters</u>

1 <u>foot</u>

Copy the grocery list below. Write your numbers and tall letters twice as high as your small letters. Keep your lines straight.

5 lb rice
8 oz cottage cheese
1 gal milk
2 L apple juice

Writing a Recipe

What is the difference between the two words at the right? Of course, one is larger. Yet, in each word, the small letters are half the size of the tall letters. This shows that the letters are in correct proportion.

In the recipe card below, the ingredients are written in adult proportion. The capital letters do not touch the top line but the small letters are still half the size of the tall letters.

tomato

tomato

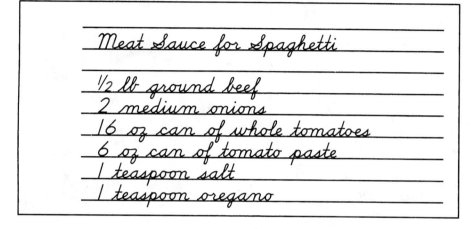

Meat Sauce for Spaghetti

½ lb ground beef
2 medium onions
16 oz can of whole tomatoes
6 oz can of tomato paste
1 teaspoon salt
1 teaspoon oregano

Copy the recipe on the card below. Plan your space so that each ingredient fits on one line. Use adult proportion.

Look at what you have written. Circle a word that has tall letters and small letters. Did you make the small letters half the size of your tall letters?

Writing Ordinal Numbers

Ordinal numbers tell in what order or position things belong. They can be written as words or as numbers and letters combined. The ordinal numbers below are written in both ways. Notice that the numbers are not joined to the letters.

1st	first	6th	sixth
2nd	second	7th	seventh
3rd	third	8th	eighth
4th	fourth	9th	ninth
5th	fifth	10th	tenth

The phrases below are missing an ordinal number. Show two ways that you can complete each phrase. Do not join numbers to letters. Use a different ordinal number for each phrase. The first one is done for you.

made it on the _____ try

5th   *fifth*

won _____ place

played _____ base

practiced it for the _____ time

sat in the _____ row

climbed to the _____ floor

68

Join lower-case letters whenever you write in cursive. Remember that some capital cursive letters are joined to the lower-case letters that follow them.

Carla and her friends organized some games for the younger children in the neighborhood. She wrote a list to show how each child placed in each game. Copy Carla's list for Maurice below. Join your letters correctly.

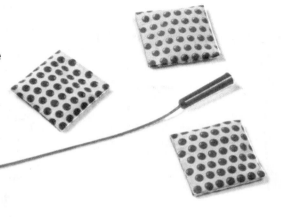

Game	Score	Place
Button in the Box	100	1st
Jump-rope Contest	22	4th
Beanbag Toss	8	6th

The message above is written in calligraphy, a style of handwriting that is very beautiful. People use calligraphy to communicate and to express their feelings at the same time.

People began to do calligraphy in China about two thousand years ago. It was used to decorate books, letters, buildings, and works of art. Calligraphy is still popular today.

People learn to do calligraphy in the same way you learn handwriting—by practicing strokes on lined paper. Look at the strokes and letters below.

You can be very inventive when you use calligraphy. Here is one way calligraphers show off their skill.

70

The instructions below tell what you need to begin learning calligraphy. Copy the two paragraphs on the lines below. Use manuscript or cursive handwriting.

To begin to learn calligraphy, you need a black felt-tip marker and lined paper with dotted midlines.

Hold your pen at a 45-degree angle so that the pen points over your shoulder. Practice writing an X on your paper. Always hold the marker in the same position. Do not press hard. If you hold the pen correctly, the X will be thick in one direction and thin in the other. Look at this example.

Are you interested in learning more about calligraphy? In a library, you'll find books that show how to practice strokes, letters, and designs. You'll also see more beautiful examples of how people use calligraphy.

Writing a Poem

In an acrostic poem, the letters in a word are used to begin each line of the poem. Each line begins with a capital letter.

Copy each poem on the lines at the right. Use either manuscript or cursive handwriting.

Peach

Pit in the center
Eat carefully around it
All juicy inside
Cool and sweet
Have another peach!

_____

_____

_____

_____

_____

_____

Grapes

Green ones
Red ones
And
Purple ones
Each grape bursting with
Such amazing flavor.

_____

_____

_____

_____

_____

_____

Letter, Word, and Sentence Spacing

What would happen if your teacher asked your class to sit in groups of three? Everyone would probably sit so there were small spaces between students and larger spaces between groups. Even spacing is important in handwriting as well.

Marta and Lawrence both wrote compositions about their heritage. Copy Marta's first paragraph below in cursive. Make even spaces between letters. Leave a larger space between words. Make more space between sentences than between words.

My mother talks to me in Spanish. It's easier for me to speak English, but I usually answer her in Spanish. Mom says it's important to learn the language of my heritage. I think, sí, it's a good idea.

Did you make even spaces between letters? Did you leave enough space between words and sentences?

Now write Lawrence's first paragraph below in cursive.
Use correct spacing.

**Cowboys, horses, and the Old West—that's what I like.
Did you know that more than one-fourth of the cowboys
were African American? My favorite black cowboy was Nat
Love. People nicknamed him "Deadwood Dick."**

Did you make even spaces between letters? between
words? between sentences?

Timed Writing

Dwayne received a call from his softball coach at the beginning of the spring season. Read what the coach said to Dwayne.

"Hi, Dwayne. This is Mr. Duff, your softball coach. I'm calling all the players to tell them that we'll start practice on Monday. That's April 22. We'll practice every Monday and Wednesday afternoon from 5:30 to 6:30 at Weiss Park. If you need to call me, my number is 555–9023. Okay?"

Use these tips when you take a telephone message.
- Ask the caller to wait until you get a pencil and paper.
- Write important information such as name, date, time, and place. Use manuscript or cursive, whichever is faster.
- Ask the caller to repeat information that you aren't sure of.

Write the message from Mr. Duff in the space below. Time your writing. Use a clock, a timer, or have a friend time you. Stop writing when four minutes are up.

_____

_____

_____

_____

_____

_____

_____

_____

Now read what you wrote. Did you write the dates, times, and numbers correctly?

Writing an Announcement

Suppose you wanted to tell people about a coming event. How would you do it? You could write an announcement. An announcement tells *what* the event is, *when* it will take place, and *where* it will be.

where and when ▶

what ▶

> *Veteran's Day Celebration*
>
> *Stop by the Media Center during the week of November 7 between 11:00 A.M. and 1:00 P.M. to join in the celebration of Veteran's Day. Our librarians, Mrs. Cortez and Mr. Phillips, have gathered together an impressive collection of informative books, photographs, and videos dedicated to this subject. Please come and honor the men and women who bravely serve our country as members of the military. Refreshments will be served.*

Imagine that you want to announce a special event such as an open house at your school, a concert, or a talent show. Write an announcement about it on the lines below. Use manuscript handwriting. Slant all your letters in the same direction.

Look over your announcement. Do your letters all slant in the same direction? Are they the correct size?

Writing Punctuation Marks

Punctuation marks help you understand the meaning of the cartoon. In fact, punctuation marks add meaning to everything you read and write. It is important to know how to form punctuation marks and where to place them. Copy the punctuation marks.

period	.	**apostrophe**	'
question mark	?	**comma**	,
exclamation mark	!	**quotation marks**	" "

When you write contractions in cursive, do not join the letters on either side of the apostrophe. Copy the words below.

can't　　　*doesn't*　　　*wouldn't*

Copy the paragraph in cursive. Make sure you place the punctuation marks in the correct position. Slant them in the same direction as the rest of your handwriting.

When I smelled smoke, I didn't wait. I called the emergency number. "My house is on fire!" I said. Then I went outside to wait for help. How's that for quick thinking?

Write your own sentence on a separate sheet of paper. Use as many punctuation marks as you can.

Writing a Journal Entry

People write in journals to keep their own record of what they think, feel, see, and do. It is important to write legibly so that later you can read what you wrote.

Just as your journal is personal, your handwriting is also personal. You show your own style in the way you slant your letters. You may slant your letters to the right or to the left. You may write straight up-and-down. Keep the same slant when you write.

Read what Khanh wrote in his journal about facing new experiences in America.

May 16, 200__

Today at the mall I saw a little boy who was afraid to get on the escalator. He reminded me of myself when I first came here from Vietnam. I was scared of escalators, the kids at school, and just about everything. Now I'm used to living here—well, almost.

In the space below, write a short list of things that little children might be afraid of. Slant your letters in the same direction.

On the lines below, write your own journal entry about something you wouldn't mind sharing. Choose a memory, your feelings, or what you did on a certain day. Some of the words below may help you start. Remember to slant all your letters in the same direction.

Now I'm not afraid of . . .

A ferocious-looking . . .

I'm the oldest so . . .

We were talking about . . .

Writing Proper Nouns

Begin proper nouns with capital letters. Remember that some capital cursive letters are not joined to the letters that follow. Look at the capital letters in the names below. They are not joined to the letters that follow them.

> ### Lunchroom Helpers for January
>
> | | | |
> |---|---|---|
> | *Brenda* | *Hannah* | *Tran* |
> | *Delia* | *Oscar* | *Val* |
> | *Frank* | *Pablo* | *Wayne* |
> | *Gerry* | *Stacy* | *Xavier* |

Write each name in the list on the lines below.

_____   _____

_____   _____

_____   _____

_____   _____

_____   _____

_____   _____

Begin titles such as Mrs., Ms., Mr., Miss, and Dr. with capital letters. If the title is also an abbreviation, end it with a period. Write the titles and names of the teachers below.

Dr. Carol Adamek   _____

Mr. Martin Red Cloud   _____

Mrs. Regina Fuller   _____

Write your name below. Give yourself a title.

_____

_____

Making Signs

Justin's grandfather taught him to make wooden signs. Justin decided to make some signs with his friends' names on them and give them to his friends as gifts. First he wrote the names large on strips of paper. When he made the wooden signs, he enlarged the names even more.

REBECCA

MR. ROH

JOEY

CHARLIE

NIEVES

DELORES

Write the names in the boxes below. Use manuscript writing. Adjust your writing to fit the space.

Writing Dates

The days of the week begin with capital letters. A period follows the abbreviation of each.

Write abbreviations for the days of the week in the form below. Adjust your writing so that it fits the space. Remember to write in a straight line.

Days of the Week

Sun.	Mon.	Tues.	Wed.	Thurs.	Fri.	Sat.

The months also begin with capital letters. So do their abbreviations. Notice that May, June, and July do not need to be abbreviated because they are short words. Look at the months below. Then write the months in the form at the right.

Months of the Year

Jan.	Feb.	Mar.
Apr.	May	June
July	Aug.	Sept.
Oct.	Nov.	Dec.

Months of the Year

Below are names of three Olympic stars and the dates they won medals. Write the dates in cursive. When you write a date, put a comma between the day and the year. Slant numbers in the same direction that you slant letters.

Michael Phelps   Aug. 21, 2004   _____

Lisa Fernandez   Aug. 23, 2004   _____

Mia Hamm   Aug. 28, 2004   _____

Below write some dates that are important to you.

_____

_____

Keeping an Assignment Book

Keeping an assignment book is a good way to remember your daily homework and future projects. You don't have to write in complete sentences. Form your letters and numbers correctly so you can easily read what you have to do.

Imagine that you must do the assignments listed on the chalkboard. Use the information to fill out the form below. Concentrate on closing letters **a, d,** and **o.** Keep your lines straight as you write.

Tues., Apr. 2 — Today's Assignments
In social studies, read pages 200–204;
draw a sod house on a prairie. Due
Wed., Apr. 3.
In reading, finish reading Teammates.
Due tomorrow.
In math, work on the Native American
Design Project. Due Fri., Apr. 26.

Name			Today's Date
Subject	**Today's Assignments**		**Date Due**

Timed Writing

Lyman decided to take notes during a class discussion about deserts. Read below what a few students in his class said.

"Rain doesn't fall very often."

"I wish I could go camping in the desert."

"Deserts look dull brown, but after a heavy rain flowers bloom."

"Some plants store their own water—like the cactus. One cactus is called the saguaro."

Use these tips when you take notes.
- Use manuscript or cursive handwriting, whichever is faster for you.
- Write down important facts and information.
- Use phrases or short sentences.

What did the students say about the desert that would be important to remember? Write notes about that information in the space below. Time your writing. Use a clock, a timer, or have a friend time you. Stop writing when four minutes are up.

_____

_____

_____

_____

_____

_____

_____

_____

Now read what you wrote. Can you understand what you wrote? Did you write important facts?

Fun with Handwriting: Fantastic Letters

Dana stared at some letters for a while. Suddenly she imagined that they turned into something else! What did letter **g** become?

If you stared at capital **M** for a while, what could it turn into?

Let your imagination go. Look at the capital and lower-case letters in the frame below. Choose one or several letters. Write them upside down, sideways, or in any direction. Use the space below to create your design or picture.

Write a title or caption in the bottom of the frame.

Writing Titles

The meaning of the first sentence at the right would be confusing if the title did not have capitals and quotation marks.

When you write the titles of books and poems, capitalize the first word and all the important words. Put quotation marks around the titles of poems. Also, underline the titles of books.

Now can you find the title of a book in the second sentence?

When I babysat for Donny, I read "I Called to the Wind" to him and he fell right to sleep.

I'm sending you Stone Fox for helping me pack all my books when I moved.

Write the book title below. Remember to underline book titles.

Nadia the Willful

Write the title of the poem below. Put quotation marks around the title of a poem.

"Our Hamster's Life"

Copy the following sentences in cursive. When you come to the title of a book or poem, rewrite it so that it is correct.

don't yell at me is a poem about how kids feel.

Remember Adan's trip to Puerto Rico in the book yagua days?

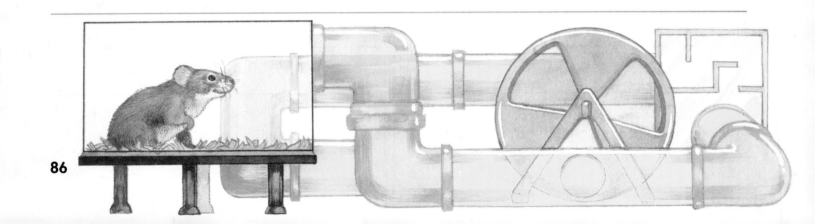

Writing a List of Favorite Books

The students in Julia's class wrote lists of books they would recommend to their classmates. They drew small pictures next to each title.

Look at the list of books and the pictures below. Find titles that match the pictures. Write the titles next to the correct pictures. Underline each title. Write small to fit each title on one line.

The Young Black Stallion   **The Phantom Tollbooth**   **My Side of the Mountain**

Below write the title of a book you would recommend to someone. You may draw a picture to go with it.

Writing a Poem

Look at the following poem. Each line begins with a capital letter, whether or not it begins a sentence. Many poems are written in this form.

Monkey Art

I taught a monkey how to draw
With a sketchpad and a pen.
It's the funniest thing you ever saw,
She's very careful, then
One mistake and she gets mad,
Out the paper goes.
She turns attention to the pad
And starts drawing with her toes!

Copy the poem in cursive on the lines below. You may have to write smaller than usual to fit each line of the poem on one writing line. Capitalize the first word in each line.

_____

_____

_____

_____

_____

_____

_____

_____

Now look at the poem below. It does not look like "Monkey Art." Can you recognize the shape of this poem? That's right—it's a moon. The shape of the poem helps us picture the idea just as the words do.

In the space at the right, copy the poem "The Changing Moon." Use manuscript handwriting.

The Changing Moon

Gaze up
    at the
        dark
            night sky
                black
                    as ink.
                        The moon
                        has lost
                        its full
                            round shape
                    and
                hangs
            like a
        shining slice

of melon.

Making a Poster

LaToya's science class studied how pollution affects the environment. They decided to make posters encouraging others to fight pollution. LaToya made one about recycling.

First she worked out her ideas on a sheet of paper, as shown below. Her paper is the same shape as the posterboard, but smaller. Notice how large she wrote the words. When LaToya makes the poster itself, she will enlarge the words to fit the size of the poster.

Lighten the garbage load . . .

Recycle!

In the space below, copy LaToya's poster or plan one of your own. Use manuscript writing. You may want to use your poster plan to make a real poster. If you do, adjust your writing to fit the large posterboard.

Writing a Thank-you Note

When you write a thank-you note in neat, legible handwriting, you show that you really mean what you say.

Your handwriting will be more legible if you always join lower-case letters when you write in cursive. Remember that some capital letters are joined to the lower-case letters that follow them, while others are not.

Study Marina's thank-you note.

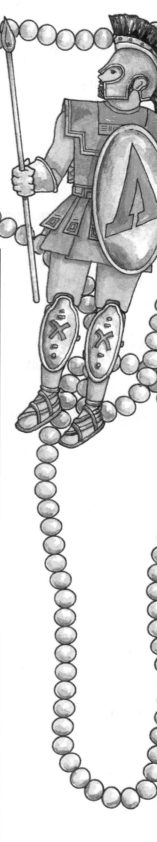

> May 24, 200_
>
> Dear Uncle Alex,
>
> Thank you for lending me your Spartan soldier doll and the worry beads. No one else brought Greek things for "Many Cultures Day" at our school! May I keep them until you visit us in July?
>
> Your niece,
> Marina

In the space below, copy the thank-you note in cursive. Remember to join lower-case cursive letters. Include the date, salutation, and closing.

Timed Writing

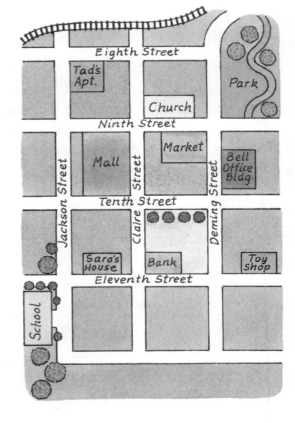

Gail just moved to a new city. She asked Rosa for directions to the park where they planned to meet after school. Rosa was in a hurry so Gail had to write quickly. Read the directions below.

"From the front of school, go left on Jackson Street to the third street. Turn right on Ninth Street. Go two blocks. You'll see the park on the left side of the street. It's at Ninth and Deming streets."

Use these tips when someone gives you directions.
- Use manuscript or cursive handwriting, whichever is faster for you.
- Write down important names and numbers.
- Ask the person to repeat anything you aren't sure of.

Imagine that you are Gail. Write the directions in the space below. Time your writing. Use a clock, a timer, or have a friend time you. Stop writing when two minutes are up.

_____

_____

_____

_____

_____

_____

_____

_____

_____

Now read what you wrote. Could you follow the directions? Did you write the names and numbers?

Writing a Science Test

Good handwriting helps you do well on science tests. It makes your words easy to read.

Getting Ready
- Read each test question carefully.
- Study any graphs or charts that are part of the question.
- Be sure you understand what to do.

Reading a Graph
- Look at the data results on the graph.
  Find the information that the question asks about.

What conclusion can you draw from the graph?
Tell how you found your answer.

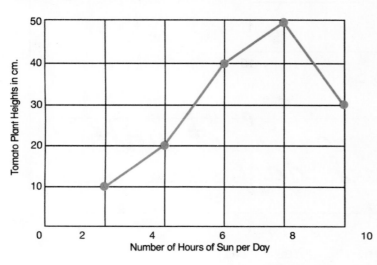

- Be sure that you answer every part of the question.
- Use your best handwriting.
  Letters should not be too close together or too far apart.
  Letters should be the correct size and proportion to fit the space.

Tomato plants need more than two hours of sun per day. I used ordered pairs on the graph.

- Review and edit your writing. Use proofreading marks to make changes or erase carefully and rewrite.

Daniel answered a question using the graph below.

What conclusion can you draw from the graph?
Tell how you found your answer.

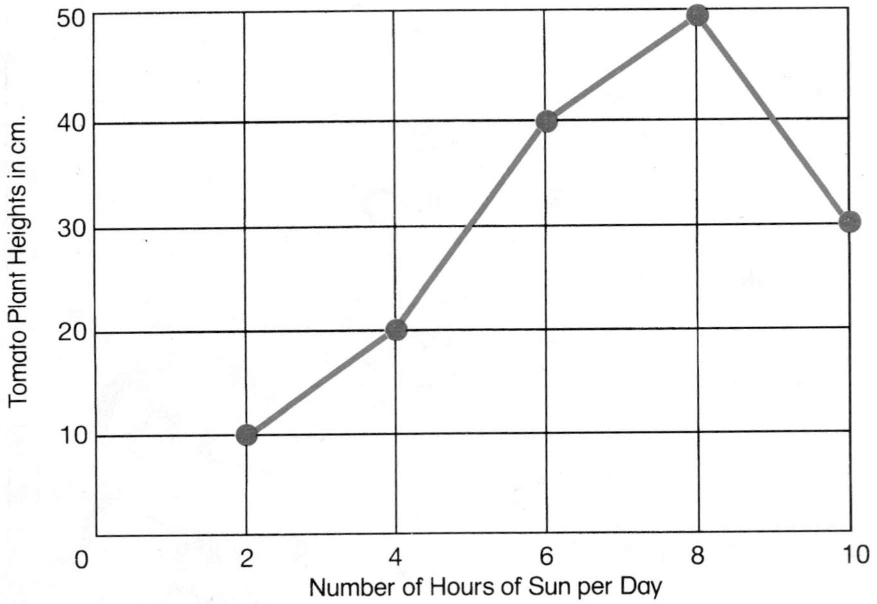
Tomato Plant Heights in cm.
50
40
30
20
10
0
2
4
6
8
10
Number of Hours of Sun per Day

Tomato plants grow best with
8 hours of sun each day.

Look at how Daniel answered the question.

	Yes	No
• Did he answer every part of the question?	☐	☐
• Are his letters the correct size and proportion to fit the space?	☐	☐

Which letters or words are not the correct size or proportion? Circle them. What part of the question is not answered? Write an answer.

Now you answer a question using the graph shown below.

What kind of light makes bean plants grow best?
Tell how you found your answer.

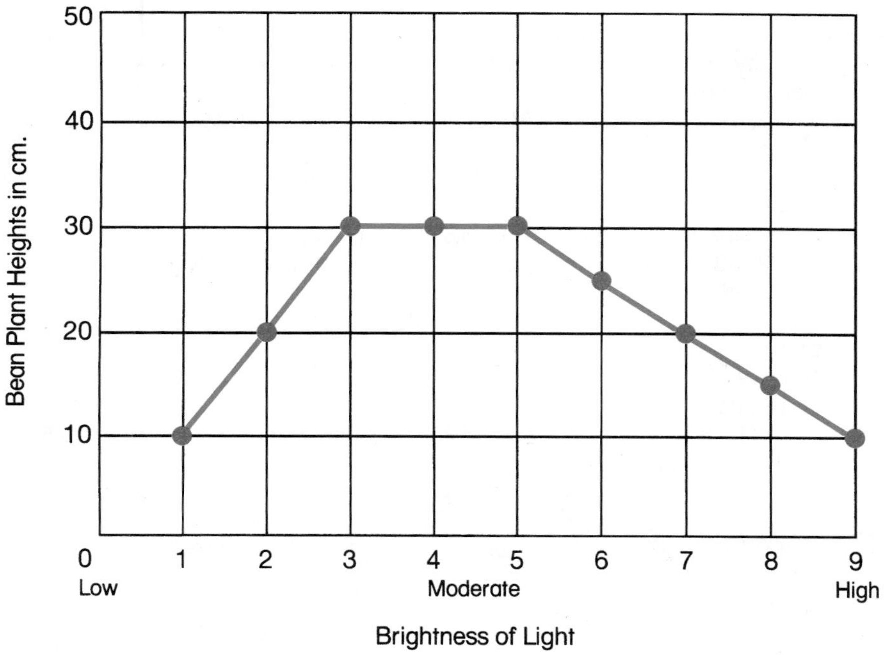

Bean Plant Heights in cm.

50
40
30
20
10

0   1   2   3   4   5   6   7   8   9
Low   Moderate   High

Brightness of Light

_____

_____

_____

_____

_____

_____

_____

_____

_____

Check your handwriting.   Yes   No
  • Did you answer every part of the question?   ☐   ☐
  • Are your letters the correct size and proportion
    to fit the space?   ☐   ☐
  • Did you fix mistakes carefully?   ☐   ☐

Circle the word you wrote best.

Index